THE SHAPING AND RESHAPING OF EARTH'S SURFACE™

Sedimentary Rocks
and the Rock Cycle

Joanne Mattern

The Rosen Publishing Group's
PowerKids Press™
New York

Published in 2006 by The Rosen Publishing Group, Inc.
29 East 21st Street, New York, NY 10010

First Edition

Editor: Melissa Acevedo
Book Design: Ginny Chu

Illustrations Credits: pp. 6, 7 by Ginny Chu

Photo Credits: Cover, p. 1 © Gabe Palmer/Corbis; p. 4 (left) Scottsdale Community College; p. 4 (right) © Kevin Schafer/Corbis; p. 8 © Paul A. Souders/Corbis; p. 11 © David Muench/Corbis; p. 12 © Pat O'Hara/Corbis; p. 13 (left) © Peter Johnson/Corbis; p. 13 (right) Kurt Hollocher, Union College Geology Department; pp. 14 (top), 17 © Maurice Nimmo; Frank Lane Picture Agency/Corbis; p. 14 (bottom) © Scott T. Smith/Corbis; pp. 16, 18 (bottom) © David Muench/Corbis; p. 18 (top) © Layne Kennedy/Corbis; p. 19 © Ric Ergenbright/Corbis; p. 20 (top right) © Archivo Iconografico, S.A./Corbis; p. 20 (top left) © Royalty-Free/Corbis; p. 20 (middle) © Larry Lee Photography/Corbis; p. 20 (bottom) © Hulton-Deutsch Collection/Corbis.

Library of Congress Cataloging-in-Publication Data

Mattern, Joanne, 1963–
Sedimentary rocks and the rock cycle / Joanne Mattern.
p. cm. — (The shaping and reshaping of Earth's surface) Includes bibliographical references and index. ISBN 1-4042-3195-1 (lib. bdg.)
1. Rocks, Sedimentary—Juvenile literature. 2. Geochemical cycles—Juvenile literature. I. Title. II. Series.
QE471.M3396 2006
552'.5—dc22

2004023030

Manufactured in the United States of America

Contents

The sediment that forms a certain sedimentary rock affects what the rock will look like. For example, arkose, shown at left, was formed mostly from pebbles. For this reason it looks like pebbles stuck together.

Do you put salt on your food? The salt that we use every day is made from a sedimentary rock called halite. Halite is formed deep under the ground.

Right:
This is a close-up picture of the sedimentary rock halite.

Sedimentary Rocks

What Is Sedimentary Rock?

Earth is made of rock that is constantly changing. These rocks, which come in different colors and sizes, help shape the surface of Earth. All the rocks on Earth belong to one of three different groups. These groups are igneous rocks, sedimentary rocks, and metamorphic rocks.

Most sedimentary rocks are made when mud, sand, or bits of rock are pressed together to form sediment. As the bits of sediment pile on top of each other, they form layers. Over time the weight of the top layers creates pressure on the lower layers and presses them together. As a result the layers become sedimentary rocks.

Most sedimentary rocks are made when mud, sand, or bits of rock are pressed together to form sediment.

Sedimentary Rocks in the Rock Cycle

The process of sediment forming sedimentary rocks is part of the rock cycle. The rock cycle is the process by which rocks are formed and then broken down through the aid of wind, water, and other forces. Over time pressure and other forces help the rock pieces and bits of other matter become new rocks.

The process by which the rock cycle creates new rocks happens in Earth's layers. It begins when the layer called the mantle pushes magma, or hot liquid rock, to Earth's surface. There the magma cools and hardens into igneous rocks. Over time

- Crust
- Inner Core
- Outer Core
- Mantle (Magma)

Earth is made up of several layers. The top layer is made of rock. It is called the crust. Under the crust is a layer of hot liquid called magma. Below the magma is Earth's core, which is made up of two layers. The outer layer is made up of melted metals. The inner layer is a solid metal ball.

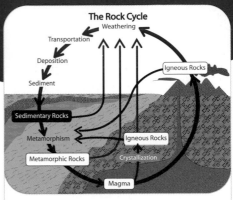

The Rock Cycle

This diagram shows the changing of old rocks into new ones through the rock cycle. Sedimentary rocks form when a lot of pressure is applied to sediment.

forces like water wear down the igneous rocks. These rock bits will form layers and be pressed together to create sedimentary rocks. Metamorphic rocks form when pressure and heat change the minerals in igneous and sedimentary rocks. Movements like earthquakes push the three kinds of rocks below Earth's crust. Magma melts these rocks and then rises to the surface to create new rocks again. Sedimentary rocks give the rock cycle the rock bits needed to create new rocks. Without these rocks the cycle could not exist.

The rock cycle is the process by which rocks are formed and then broken down through the aid of wind, water, and other forces.

Sedimentary rocks are softer than igneous and metamorphic rocks. Because of this they weather a lot more quickly. Sedimentary rocks also weather faster than other rocks because most are arranged in layers that break apart very easily.

Right:
This picture, taken in 1994, shows eroded sandstone at the Dinosaur Provincial Park in Alberta, Canada.

How Sedimentary Rocks Are Formed

Weathering

Sedimentary rocks are strong, but forces like water can wear them down during a process called weathering. There are two types of weathering. Physical weathering occurs when physical forces wear down a rock. For example, wind can blow bits of matter against a sedimentary rock, breaking it down over time. Chemical weathering occurs when elements, such as water, change a rock's minerals into different minerals. Elements are added or removed from the minerals, which weakens the rock. This occurs when minerals in sedimentary rocks absorb water. The water breaks down the rock from the inside.

Elements are added or removed from the minerals, which weakens the rock.

Erosion

After rocks are worn down through weathering, they are often broken down into even smaller pieces. As part of the rock cycle, these pieces travel through water and wind. Bits of rock, grains of sand, and other matter mix in with them to create sediment. Erosion is the process rocks go through of wearing away, traveling, and being deposited, or left behind, to form sediment.

Once the sediment has formed, it travels through various streams and rivers. The waves in the water move the sediment around. Sediment is heavier than water, so it sinks to the bottom. The largest and heaviest pieces of sediment fall through the water quickly. Lighter pieces settle on top of the heavier ones. The very lightest pieces settle on the top layer. Sediment is always washing into the ocean and adding new layers.

The Mississippi River dumps about 220 million tons (199,580,643 t) of new sediment into the Gulf of Mexico every year.

Many different things can cause erosion. Rainwater falls against sedimentary rocks, washing away the already weak and weathered pieces. These rock pieces then get swept up by the water into rivers and streams. In time they end up settling into layers at the bottom of the ocean. Both weathering and erosion have important roles in the creation of sedimentary rocks. They help create and move sediment. Without sediment most sedimentary rocks would not be able to form.

Erosion is the process rocks go through of wearing away, traveling, and being deposited, or left behind, to form sediment.

Pressure

If you lay a book flat on your hand, it might not feel very heavy. However, when you add another book, you add more weight. If you keep adding books, the pile gets heavier and the pressure on your hand increases. This pile of books is like layers of sediment. Both are under major pressure.

The Grand Canyon formed millions of years ago when the Colorado River eroded layers of sedimentary rock. The layers of sediment in the Grand Canyon are clearly visible. This makes it an excellent example of the lithification process and how rock layers form over time. The rock layers at the bottom are judged to be about one billion years old!

Lithification is the process in which pressure is applied to layers of sediment and its minerals to create new sedimentary rocks. Pressure must be applied to the layers over millions of years. The process begins when layers of sediment are added to the bottom layers

These beach pebbles have already been smoothed by water.

Over time the pebbles join other matter to form a conglomerate rock.

through erosion. The added layers put more pressure on the bottom layer of sediment. This pressure pushes out any water that may be in the sediment. Taking out the water makes it easier for the minerals in the sediment to be pushed together. When the minerals are pushed together, they change and harden. This makes it easier to form sedimentary rocks. Over millions of years, the layers of sediment harden into a sedimentary rock. The layers of sediment have to be about ½ mile (1 km) to 2 miles (3 km) deep to create enough pressure to form sedimentary rock.

Lithification is the process in which pressure is applied to layers of sediment and its minerals to create new sedimentary rocks.

Breccia rocks got their name from the Latin word meaning "broken." Breccia forms at the bottom of a sloping area, like a hill, where loose rocks have gathered. Breccia's color depends on the color of the rock pieces that created it.

Conglomerates are made of rounded pebbles. They are then stuck together through the process of lithification with other kinds of sediment, such as sand or clay. Water moves over the pebbles to wear away the edges. The water makes them smooth and round.

Right:
This conglomerate is located in the Wasatch Mountains in Utah.

CONTENT SKILL: Kinds of Sedimentary Rock: Clastic Rocks

Kinds of Sedimentary Rocks

Clastic Rocks

There are three groups of sedimentary rocks. Clastic rocks are the largest. They are made up of clasts which are bits of rock and matter like mud. Like other sedimentary rocks, clastic rocks are formed from layers of sediment under pressure.

Conglomerates are clastic rocks made of smooth pebbles. They are formed through the process of lithification, which can take thousands of years. Breccia, another clastic rock, is also formed from rocks stuck together. Unlike those in conglomerates, the rocks in breccia are sharp and rough. The rocks that form breccia did not travel in water long enough to become smooth.

Like other sedimentary rocks, clastic rocks are formed when layers of sediment are under pressure.

Chemically Formed Rocks

Most sedimentary rocks are formed from layers of sediment under pressure. However, some sedimentary rocks form when minerals break down in water. This type of sedimentary rock is chemically formed.

Mammoth Cave in Kentucky is the longest cave in the world. The cave covers more than 340 miles (547 km). There are many stalactites and stalagmites inside!

Have you ever seen the inside of a cave? There are rocks hanging from the ceiling and standing up from the floor. These stalactites and stalagmites are chemically formed sedimentary rocks. Caves are often made of a sedimentary rock called limestone. Limestone contains a mineral called calcite. When water seeps through limestone, it breaks down the calcite. In time the water

Geodes are hollow, round sedimentary rocks formed from sediment. When opened, you can see the layer of agate inside.

disappears leaving behind a calcite deposit. The calcite deposit hardens into rocks. Stalagmites form from the calcite deposit that builds up and drips onto the floor of a cave. Stalactites form when the calcite hangs from the ceiling.

Sometimes water collects in small holes in the ground. If a mineral called quartz is in these holes, a sedimentary rock called agate can form. The water breaks down the quartz and creates agate. Agate forms in layers and is very smooth. Agate often forms inside geodes.

Chemically formed sedimentary rocks are different from other rocks because they have different minerals.

Organically Formed Rocks

This picture shows a fossilized starfish in a sedimentary rock.

An organic rock is formed from fossils, or the remains of dead creatures. The bottom of a lake or an ocean is covered with shells of very tiny sea animals that lived there millions of years ago. Over time these shells can be pushed down by the layers of sediment above them. Some of these shells contain calcite, which forms a sedimentary rock called limestone. Limestone is usually white, gray, or black. Sometimes you can see tiny pieces of shells inside a piece of a limestone rock. These shell pieces are so small that they can only be

If you want to tell if a rock is limestone, pour some vinegar over it. Most limestone will bubble if it touches vinegar. Vinegar is a sour liquid used in cooking.

This picture of the White Cliffs of Dover in Kent, England, was taken in 1990. The cliffs are well known for their white, chalky appearance.

seen under a microscope. Chalk is a kind of limestone rock. Limestone chalk can form giant cliffs, like the White Cliffs of Dover in England.

Many sedimentary rocks contain fossils. Most plants and animals rot away or are eaten by other animals. However, if a plant or an animal is buried quickly by sediment, it can become a fossil. Fossils in a rock can tell scientists which creatures lived on Earth millions of years ago.

Fossils in a rock can tell scientists which creatures lived on Earth millions of years ago.

Chalk is made of limestone. People write on blackboards with chalk.

These flint weapons were found in San Giorgio di Nogaro, Italy.

Coal, a sedimentary rock, is easy to burn. It is also a good source of heat.

CONTENT SKILL: Uses of Sedimentary Rocks

People used the sedimentary rock limestone to build pyramids in ancient Egypt. This pyramid, at the right, is known as the Great Pyramid. It was built in Egypt around 2600 B.C.

Right:
Scientists believe that it took about 20 years to build the Great Pyramid.

Uses of Sedimentary Rocks

Useful Sedimentary Rocks

Many sedimentary rocks are useful. For example, limestone is often used for building. Famous churches, such as Notre Dame in Paris, France, are made from limestone. Limestone can be heated and ground into cement.

You may have seen trucks spreading rock salt to melt ice and snow in the winter. Rock salt is made from sedimentary rocks.

Coal is a sedimentary rock that is made of plants. When plants waste away, they become sediment. Pressure changes the sediment into coal. At one time buildings all over the world were heated by coal. People in ancient times used a sedimentary rock called flint to make tools. They also rubbed together pieces of flint to start a fire.

At one time buildings all over the world were heated by coal.

The Importance of Sedimentary Rocks

Sedimentary rocks are also important to scientists. Scientists can study sedimentary rocks to see the layers of sediment that formed them. Studying the rock layers helps scientists discover how Earth formed and how much it has changed over the years. Sedimentary rocks also hold clues to how old Earth really is. Fossils trapped in these rocks tell scientists which creatures lived on Earth millions of years ago. Scientists can also study sedimentary rocks from different parts of the world to see what Earth looked like long ago.

The rock cycle has helped shape Earth for millions of years. Being a part of the rock cycle, sedimentary rocks are important in the shaping of Earth's surface. Without sedimentary rocks Earth would be a very different place.

absorb (ub-ZORB) To take in and hold on to something.

chemical (KEH-mih-kul) Having to do with changes caused by mixing matter.

conglomerates (kun-GLOM-rets) Types of sedimentary rocks made of rounded rock pieces that are stuck together.

deposit (dih-PAH-zit) Something that is left behind.

earthquakes (URTH-kwayks) Shakings of Earth's surface caused by the movement of large pieces of land that run into each other.

erosion (ih-ROH-zhun) The breaking down and moving of rocks and other matter by natural forces.

igneous rocks (IG-nee-us ROKS) Hot, liquid, underground minerals that have cooled and hardened into rocks.

lithification (lih-thuh-fuh-KAY-shun) The process of changing layers of sediment into sedimentary rock.

metamorphic rocks (meh-tuh-MOR-fik ROKS) Rocks that have been changed by heat and heavy weight.

minerals (MIN-rulz) Natural elements that are not animals, plants, or other living things.

physical (FIH-zih-kul) Having to do with natural forces.

sediment (SEH-deh-ment) Sand, or mud carried by wind or water.

sedimentary rocks (seh-deh-MEN-teh-ree ROKS) Layers of gravel, sand, or mud that have been pressed together to form rocks.

stalactites (stuh-LAK-tyts) Creations made by water and rock that hang down from the ceilings of caves.

stalagmites (stuh-LAG-myts) Creations made by water and rock that rise up from the ground.

weathering (WEH-thur-ing) The breaking down of rocks through natural forces.

Index

A
agate, 17

B
breccia, 15

C
calcite, 16–18
chemical weathering, 9
coal, 21
conglomerates, 15

E
earthquakes, 7

I
igneous rocks, 5–7

L
limestone, 16, 18–19, 21

lithification, 12

M
metamorphic rocks, 5, 7

N
Notre Dame, 21

P
physical weathering, 9

S
sediment, 5–6, 10–13, 16,
    18–19, 21–22
stalactites, 16–17
stalagmites, 16–17

W
White Cliffs of Dover, 19

Web Sites

Due to the changing nature of Internet links, PowerKids Press has developed an online list of Web sites related to the subject of this book. This site is updated regularly. Please use this link to access the list: www.powerkidslinks.com/sres/sediment/